Here's the sun!

Here's a rainbow!

Activities

1 Colour Colin.

2 Find and circle
Colin's friends.

14

Picture Dictionary

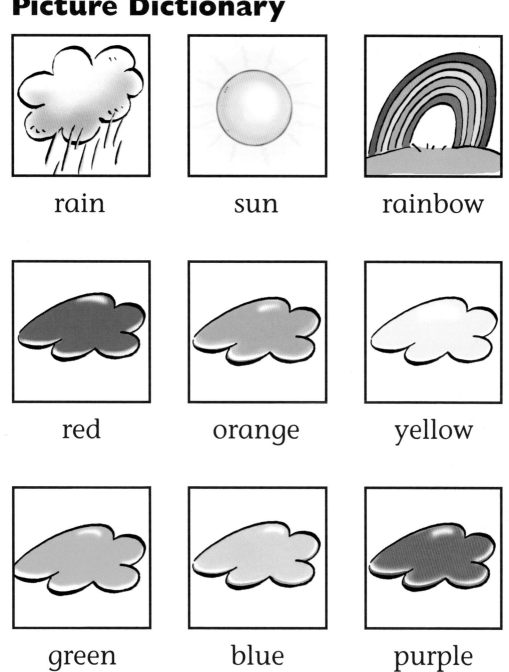

rain

sun

rainbow

red

orange

yellow

green

blue

purple

Macmillan Education
Between Towns Road, Oxford OX4 3PP
A division of Macmillan Publishers Limited
Companies and representatives throughout the world

ISBN-13: 978 1 4050 2500 3
ISBN-13: 978 1 4050 5717 2 (International Edition)
ISBN-10: 1 4050 2500 X
ISBN-10: 1 4050 5717 3 (International Edition)

Illustrated by Gloria Celma

Printed and bound in Spain by Mateu Cromo

2008 2007 2006
10 9 8 7 6 5   Spain
10 9 8 7 6 5   International